# DISCOVER THE CONTINENTS

# Europe

by Emily Rose Oachs

BLASTOFF!
3
READERS

BELLWETHER MEDIA • MINNEAPOLIS, MN

Note to Librarians, Teachers, and Parents:

**Blastoff! Readers** are carefully developed by literacy experts and combine standards-based content with developmentally appropriate text.

**Level 1** provides the most support through repetition of high-frequency words, light text, predictable sentence patterns, and strong visual support.

**Level 2** offers early readers a bit more challenge through varied simple sentences, increased text load, and less repetition of high-frequency words.

**Level 3** advances early-fluent readers toward fluency through increased text and concept load, less reliance on visuals, longer sentences, and more literary language.

**Level 4** builds reading stamina by providing more text per page, increased use of punctuation, greater variation in sentence patterns, and increasingly challenging vocabulary.

**Level 5** encourages children to move from "learning to read" to "reading to learn" by providing even more text, varied writing styles, and less familiar topics.

Whichever book is right for your reader, Blastoff! Readers are the perfect books to build confidence and encourage a love of reading that will last a lifetime!

This edition first published in 2017 by Bellwether Media, Inc.

No part of this publication may be reproduced in whole or in part without written permission of the publisher. For information regarding permission, write to Bellwether Media, Inc., Attention: Permissions Department, 6012 Blue Circle Dr., Minnetonka, MN 55343.

Library of Congress Cataloging-in-Publication Data

Oachs, Emily Rose.
  Europe / by Emily Rose Oachs.
    pages cm – (Blastoff! Readers: Discover the Continents)
  Includes bibliographical references and index.
  Summary: "Simple text and full-color photography introduce beginning readers to Europe. Developed by literacy experts for students in kindergarten through third grade"– Provided by publisher.
  Audience: Grades K-3.
  ISBN 978-1-62617-327-9 (hardcover : alk. paper)
  ISBN 978-1-61891-258-9 (paperback : alk. paper)
  1. Europe–Juvenile literature. I. Title.
  D1051.O23 2016
  914–dc23
                         2015028726

Printed in the United States of America, North Mankato, MN.

# Table of Contents

# Small Continent, Large Population

Colosseum

Many people live in Europe. It is the second-smallest **continent** in **area**. But it has the third-largest **population**.

# DID YOU KNOW?

- Ancient Greece was an early society that came up with important ideas that the world still uses today.

- In Venice, Italy, waterways flow through the city instead of streets. People take boats to get to places.

- Vatican City is a country that is smaller than New York City's Central Park!

- The Bosporus River divides Istanbul, Turkey into both Europe and Asia.

**Bosporus River**

The Colosseum is a famous **landmark** in Italy. In France, the Eiffel Tower looks out over Paris.

# Where Is Europe?

To Europe's north is the Arctic Ocean. The Atlantic Ocean lies to Europe's west. To its south is the Mediterranean Sea. Asia borders eastern Europe.

The **prime meridian** passes through Europe. This places Europe in the Western, Eastern, and Northern **hemispheres**.

# The Land and Climate

Alps

Low **plains** cover much of Europe. Forests and **tundra** blanket the north.

Some mountains rise in Europe. The Alps cross central Europe. The Pyrenees separate Spain and France. Europe's eastern border in Russia is made by the Urals.

Pyrenees

Ural Mountains

Alps

Pyrenees

N
W E
S

Warm Atlantic winds blow across Europe. This gives much of the continent **mild** weather.

Arctic
Circle

N
W E
S

Arctic Circle

On southern coasts, summers
are hot and winters are mild.
Winters inside the **Arctic Circle**
are cold and long.

# The Plants and Animals

tulip field

edelweiss

White edelweiss flowers dot the Alps. In the spring, tulips bloom in Dutch fields.

Cypress and olive trees grow near the Mediterranean Sea. In the north, spruce and fir forests are common.

fir forest

cypress trees

Seals dive in the Mediterranean Sea. Puffins nest along the Atlantic Ocean's rocky coasts. In forests, wolves and lynx hunt **prey**. Nightingales sing from trees.

seal

puffins

nightingale

lynx

reindeer

Each winter, northern reindeer **migrate** south. They search for food.

# The People

There are 47 countries in Europe. About 741 million people call Europe home.

Russia spreads over Europe and Asia. No European country has more people. About 110 million people live in Russia's European side.

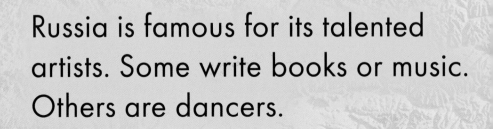

Russia is famous for its talented artists. Some write books or music. Others are dancers.

Europe has always been a leader in art. Many painters, musicians, and authors have come from many of its countries. People around the world enjoy their art.

# Fast Facts About Europe

**Size:** 4 million square miles (10.4 million square kilometers); 2nd smallest continent

**Number of Countries:** 47

**Largest Country:** Russia

**Smallest Country:** Vatican City

**Number of People:** 741 million people

**Place with Most People:** Russia

**Top Natural Resources:** wood, coal, oil, natural gas, livestock

**Top Landmarks:**
- Big Ben (London, United Kingdom)
- Eiffel Tower (Paris, France)
- Colosseum (Rome, Italy)
- Acropolis (Athens, Greece)
- St. Basil's Cathedral (Moscow, Russia)

Big Ben

St. Basil's Cathedral

Russia

N
W · E
S

Vatican City

Acropolis

Eiffel Tower

Colosseum

# Glossary

**Arctic Circle**—the northernmost part of the world

**area**—a region's size

**continent**—one of the seven main land areas on Earth; the continents are Africa, Antarctica, Asia, Australia, Europe, North America, and South America.

**hemispheres**—halves of the globe; the equator and prime meridian divide Earth into different hemispheres.

**landmark**—an important structure or place

**migrate**—to travel from one place to another, often with the seasons

**mild**—not too hot or too cold

**plains**—large areas of flat land

**population**—the number of people who live in an area

**prey**—animals that are hunted by other animals for food

**prime meridian**—an imaginary line that runs vertically through Earth; the prime meridian divides the planet into a western half and an eastern half.

**tundra**—frozen, treeless land

# To Learn More

**AT THE LIBRARY**
Cooper, Sharon Katz. *Gustave Eiffel's Spectacular Idea: The Eiffel Tower.* North Mankato, Minn.: Picture Window Books, 2016.

Kalman, Bobbie. *Spotlight on Russia.* New York, N.Y.: Crabtree Pub. Co., 2011.

Oxlade, Chris. *Introducing Europe.* Chicago, Ill.: Capstone Heinemann Library, 2014.

**ON THE WEB**
Learning more about Europe is as easy as 1, 2, 3.

1. Go to www.factsurfer.com.

2. Enter "Europe" into the search box.

3. Click the "Surf" button and you will see a list of related web sites.

With factsurfer.com, finding more information is just a click away.

# Index

The images in this book are reproduced through the courtesy of: Vaclav Volrab, front cover; Iakov Kalinin, p. 4; davesimon, p. 5; Anna Jedynak, p. 8; Lenar Musin, p. 9; Michele Falzone/ Age Fotostock, p. 10; valeriiaarnaud, p. 11; Artens, p. 12 (top); Xseon, p. 12 (bottom); troyka, p. 13 (top); JaroPienza, p. 13 (bottom); Michael Thaler, p. 14 (left); zaferkizilkaya, p. 14 (top right); AndreAnita, p. 14 (center right); John Navajo, p. 14 (bottom right); Bildagentur Zoonar GmbH, p. 15; IR Stone, p. 16; withGod, p. 18; Deposit Photos/ Glow Images, p. 19; QQ7, p. 21 (top left); dimbar76, p. 21 (top right); WDG Photo, p. 21 (bottom left); Nattee Chalermtiragool, p. 21 (bottom center); Egor Tetiushev, p. 21 (bottom right).